Young Learner's

LOOK-n-LEARN

TRANSPORT & COMMUNICATION

Transport

Airplane

An airplane flies in the sky. It is the fastest means of travel across cities, countries and continents. It comes in a variety of shapes and sizes.

Ambulance

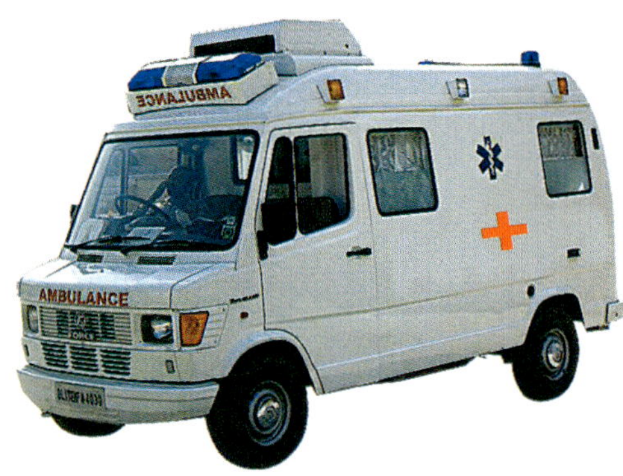

An ambulance is an emergency van that transports injured or ill people to the hospital. It has a red cross on it.

Auto-rickshaw

An auto-rickshaw is a covered motor vehicle with one wheel at the front and two at the back. It has a long seat at the back for passengers.

Bicycle

A bicycle is a vehicle with two wheels. It is ridden by pushing its pedals forward. It is an environment-friendly form of transport.

Bulldozer

A bulldozer is a construction vehicle. It has a large metal plate in the front to move soil or sand and to knock down buildings.

Bus

A bus is a vehicle for public transport and travels along a fixed route. It can seat many people and is one of the most common means of transport.

Cable car

A cable car can transport people across seas or through mountains. It moves along a cable fixed between two points of travel.

Canoe

A canoe is a light boat that narrows at both ends. It can be moved along in water by using a paddle. The first known canoe factory was built in 1750.

Car

A car is a road vehicle with four wheels. It is driven by a diesel or petrol engine. It can carry only a small number of passengers.

Cogwheel train

A cogwheel train is a train fitted with cogwheels. These trains run in mountain areas. The first cog railway was the Mount Washington Cog Railway.

Crane

A crane is used to lift and lower materials, and transport them from one place to another. It can pick up heavy loads easily.

Cruise

A cruise liner is a large ship that carries people mainly for holiday purposes. It has many rooms, swimming pool, entertainment centre, etc. on board.

Dog sled

A dog sled is a vehicle pulled by dogs. It slides over snow. Sled dogs can run at a speed of 30 km/h. It is mainly used in Canada and Alaska.

Ferry

A ferry is used for short-distance travelling by sea. It can carry many passengers, small vehicles and cargo. It is also called a water bus or water taxi.

Forklift truck

A forklift truck has a special equipment on the front that can move and lift heavy objects. It is commonly seen at construction sites.

Gondola

A gondola is a long boat used on canals in Venice. It has a flat bottom and high parts at both ends. Gondolas are handmade and the oars are made of beechwood.

Helicopter

A helicopter has large blades on top that go round. It is used to transport a small number of people across long distances.

Hot air balloon

A hot air balloon is a large balloon with a basket to carry passengers. It is filled with hot air or gas that makes it rise in the air.

Lorry

A lorry is a large road vehicle used to transport heavy loads. It has a long covered compartment for keeping the goods.

Metro

A metro is an underground train that runs on electricity. It is a quick means of transport between various parts of a city.

Mixer

A mixer is a construction vehicle. It is used to mix large quantities of concrete or cement with water. It was invented by Gebhardt Jaeger.

Motorbike

A motorbike is a vehicle with two wheels. It is driven by an engine. It has two seats, one for the rider and the other for the passenger.

Motorboat

A motorboat is a small boat powered by an engine. It can move at quick speeds across a water body. It is also called a powerboat.

Parachute

A parachute is a device used to land people, goods or supplies slowly and safely when they are dropped from an aircraft.

Police van

A police van is a vehicle used by police officers to transport criminals to the police station or to jail. It may have a wire shield across the windscreen.

Quad bike

A quad bike has four wheels. It can travel on rough paths. It is often used for sports like off-road races. It has a weight of about 550 kg.

Road roller

A road roller has a large roller in the front of the vehicle. It smoothens the concrete on the roads. The first rollers were drawn by horses.

Rowboat

A rowboat is a small boat that is moved using oars. It is also called a rowing boat. An 8 feet rowboat uses a 6½ feet oar.

Sailboat

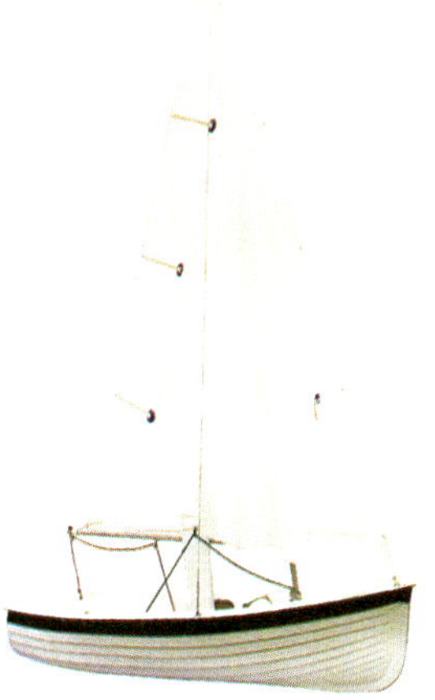

A sailboat is used to sail out into the sea. It has a giant sail that uses the power of the wind to move. It is smaller than a sailing ship.

Scooter

A scooter is a vehicle with two wheels. It usually has a curved metal cover at the front to protect the rider's legs. It is also known as kick scooter.

Skateboard

A skateboard is a short narrow board with small wheels at each end. The board is used to stand on and ride as a sport.

Snowmobile

A snowmobile can easily move over ice and snow. It is used for transportation in snowy regions. It has skis in the front to control direction of travel.

Spacecraft

A spacecraft is used to travel from Earth into space. It is used for the transportation of humans and cargo, communications, etc.

Submarine

A submarine is an underwater boat. It is mainly used by the military. It can stay underwater for as long as six months.

Tanker

A tanker is a big road vehicle. It is used to transport large quantities of liquids like water, oil, milk, and gases by road.

Taxi

A taxi is a vehicle for hire along with a driver. The world's first motorised taxi was built in 1897 and was called the Daimler Victoria.

Tractor

A tractor is driven by a farmer on the farm. Early tractors were steam driven but now they are powered by gasoline or diesel engine.

Train

A train runs on tracks laid on fixed routes between cities and towns. It can carry passengers and cargo over long distances.

Tram

A tram runs on rail tracks along the streets. It is a common mode of transport in many countries. It is used to carry both passengers and freight.

Tricycle

A tricycle is a small vehicle with one wheel at the front and two at the back. It is generally ridden by small children. It was invented in Germany in 1680.

Trishaw

A trishaw is a light vehicle with three wheels. It is moved by pushing its pedals. It has space for two or three passengers.

Trolleybus

A trolleybus is an electric bus that gets electricity from the wires located overhead. It runs on a track. It is an environment-friendly means of transport.

Van

A van is a covered vehicle with no windows in the back half. It is used for carrying goods or people. It comes in many different shapes and sizes.

Yacht

A yacht is a boat used mainly for leisure. It can sail fast across the sea. Some yachts have fully furnished rooms on them.

Communication

Email

An email is an electronic letter. It is used to send instant messages, including graphic images and sound files, anywhere in the world through the Internet.

Facsimile

A facsimile is commonly called a fax. It is a device used for transmitting an exact copy of a document, photograph, etc. by means of a telephone.

Internet

Internet is an international computer network. It is used for searching and sharing information among billions of users across the world.

Journal

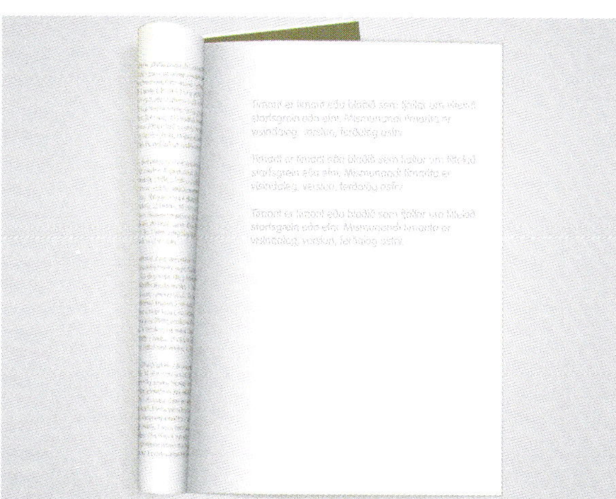

A journal is a magazine or newspaper that deals with a particular profession or subject. The different types of journals are scientific, trade, travel, etc.

Letter

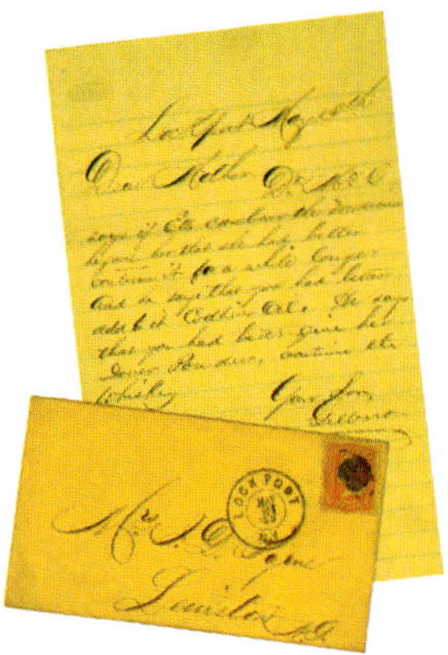

A letter is a message written on a paper and put into an envelope. The envelope bearing the address of the receiver is put in a mailbox from where it is collected by a postman.

Magazine

A magazine is a number of pages bound together. A wide variety of magazines on different subjects like politics, business, fashion, etc. are printed worldwide.

Morse code

Morse code is a way of sending a message using a series of tones, lights or clicks to represent numbers and letters of the alphabet. First Morse Code message was sent on May 24, 1844.

Newspaper

A newspaper is made of sheets of paper put together and giving information about happenings around the world. It may be printed daily, weekly or even monthly.

Pager

A pager is a wireless electronic device that displays text messages and plays voice messages from others. Two-way pagers can also reply or create new messages.

Radar

A radar is an object detecting system. It uses radio waves to locate the position and movement of objects like ships and planes when they cannot be seen.

Radio

A radio broadcasts many channels including sports, news, music, etc. Voice was first sent by radio waves in 1906. FM radio made its first appearance in 1939.

Satellite

A satellite is a device sent into space to move around Earth or another planet. It enables communication by radio, television, etc. Sputnik 1, launched in 1957, was the first satellite.

Smartphone

A smartphone can be used for calling, texting, mailing, sharing photos and videos and many other purposes.

Telegraph

A telegraph is an old means of sending urgent messages quickly. Generally, short messages were sent through it.

Telephone

A telephone is a device to have voice conversations with people. The first practical telephone was invented by Graham Bell.

Television

A television broadcasts news, sports and entertainment programmes. The first television was invented in 1927 by J.L. Baird.